To order additional copies of this book, contact:
Xlibris
844-714-8691
www.Xlibris.com
Orders@Xlibris.com

ISBN: Softcover   978-1-6641-4281-7
       EBook   978-1-6641-4280-0

Print information available on the last page

Rev. date: 11/13/2020

Noaella's

Children's Christian Poems

Noaella Eley-Bryant

Dedication

First, I would like to praise God for the over flowing ideas that came into my mind all at once, after talking to my onsite pastor about her book. I was actually going to see her about something totally different, when she shared with me about having writer block, while she was writing her fourth book, and asked me to pray with her. I did and God came through for her. But before I knew her results, I slipped in the thought of me having writers' block. I was currently working on my four-book series, "The Power of Chemistry", and other projects, as if that wasn't enough information flowing in my head already. Before I knew it, I said, "So that is it God. You are just going to let me have writer's block one day. I write some books and then get stuck. Is that it, huh, just stuck with nothing else to write". I don't know why I was letting it get to me like that. Now that I think about it, it was all quite funny. But all of a sudden, flashes of this book that I have written, flashed right before me, really fast, and detailed. I saw a lot of different children popping up in my mind, with different instruments, explaining how they would praise the Lord, with rhyming words to it. It was amazing. It was excellent. I knew that this book would be an example and an encouragement for children, and teach them how to worship God. Then I knew I had to repent to God for being so hasty to jump to conclusion, and for not having strong faith. I thank my onsite Pastor Laura Mittchell, because if it hadn't been for talking with her that day, I wouldn't have gotten the chance to peek into my future about this book.

I would like to give thanks to my grandchildren for being my first audiences for my children books, and showing me how much they enjoy the poems. They absolutely love my first children's book, " Noaella's Children's Poems", and I know they will really enjoy this book too. I love you dearly Erainiesha Price, Darrell Patterson Jr.,

Destiny Cathey, Layla Cathey, and Lyric Cathey. Thanks for being there for your grandmother. And special thanks for Destiny, Layla, and Lyric Cathey for being a model in my book. They are really having a great time with the instruments they got to keep.

Thanks to Sister Dianne Hunter, my friend that would always make sure I had children to Photograph for this book and my other book, "The Power of Chemistry Part 4." She even let her granddaughters Da'mara, Danielle and her grandsons Courtney and Ethen participate in it. She has really been a blessing to me. Also, a lot of thanks to Sister Rosslon Clayton and her husband David Clayton Sr., that let their son David Jr., be a part of this book and, "The Power of Chemistry Part 4." Special thanks to my friend Regina Sanders, for letting her granddaughter Corri Sanders posed in my book. More thanks to my friend Erica Thomas for also letting her daughter Enya Thomas to be photographed in my book. And a very special thanks to my daughter Kendra Jefferson, which is my very special supermodel. She always tells me that when we go for a Photo Shoot, for one of my books or for one of the outfits I crocheted. She does a really good job and she looks so beautiful on the fount cover of this book. And I would like to thank everyone else that was a part of this book. I really appreciate you.

Now my mother is residing with the Lord in heaven, but I am very thankful for the time she took to raise me, and help me use and develop my gifts and talents from the Lord. She helped me flourish them into great work. I will never have another mom, and I missed her very much, but I know God is taking really good care of her, and there is no more pain and discomfort. I love you mom.

My Praise to The Lord

I praise the Lord playing the guitar

I'm not at home playing with an avatar

My music I play is as sweet as me

I will be in heaven where the angels will be

Praise with a Sound

I praise my God playing my drums

I pray that no one I know will ever be a bum

Being a child knowing the Lord

Everything I pray for is never void

Tambourine Praise

I step out with my tambourine

It sounds so good just like in my dreams

Every tap on it is for God

That is how I praise the Lord

My Piano

I sing and play my piano

Right in front of my friend name Brianna

All of it is worship to my Lord

And that is how I praise my God

My Tithes

I praise the Lord by tithing

I'm going to have the best car when I start driving

I pay my ten percent on all my increase

Today I'm eating fish without frying it in grease

My God supply all my needs

And I like when my hair is braided up with beads

I Read My Bible

Every day I read my Bible

I can't wait until the next revival

God want us to meditate on his word

Day and night are what I heard

And that my friend, is better than hors d'oeuvre

I Love to Play the Trumpet

I love to play the trumpet

It's better than winning a contest of romp it

The tunes that roam around your ears

It will just bring down happy tears

I play the trumpet so well

God will really be swell

Because I do it unto him

The praises come from me and my friend name Kim.

I Raise My Hands

I raise my hands to praise the Lord

Hallelujah he is my God

Raising my hands up high

Praising him and looking at the sky

He is my King and Lord of Lords

I praise him a lot because he is God

And that's how I get my praises to the Lord

God Receives My Praises

God receives my praises through my saxophone

I'm not sitting all day on my telephone

I love the way my saxophone is made

Then the tunes I made from it just fade

As I remember the day, I got saved

I'm A Big Kid

I'm a big kid playing the clarinet

I use to sleep in a bassinet

My tunes and sounds that I play

Is a gift to God as I say

Thank you for a very good day

Sending Praises

Playing the flute sending my praise

I send a toot while I'm being raised

To say my prayers before I go to bed

My favorite color is always red

Going to church having my spirit fed

Sharing the good news with my friend name Ted

Songs with My Xylophone

It is a lot of fun playing my xylophone

It is very different from playing a saxophone

Or even playing a trombone

I like to make up a song

While I praise the Lord on my xylophone

Playing My Violin

I love to play my violin

Instead of playing with my friend name Ken

My mom put all my toys in a bin

I'm singing a song call God Forgive Me of My Sin

While I'm still playing my violin

And I'm playing for real there is no pretend

Now I bowed my head to say Amen

I Praise the Lord with My Harmonica

I praise the Lord with my harmonica

Sitting there listening is my friend Monica

She loves to hear me play for hours

Then I wipe sweat from my head with a towel

Monica starts to sing her song

Oh, my goodness we are praising the Lord all day long

Noaella's Children's Christian Poems

And we all are praising the Lord with our instruments!

Printed in the United States
By Bookmasters